BOOK 1

MULTIPLE SKILLS
SERIES: Reading

Third Edition

Richard A. Boning

SRA
McGraw-Hill

Columbus, Ohio

A Division of The McGraw·Hill Companies

SRA/McGraw-Hill

*A Division of The **McGraw·Hill** Companies*

Send all inquiries to:
SRA/McGraw-Hill
8787 Orion Place
Columbus, OH 43240-4027

ISBN 0-02-688414-3

8 9 SCG 02

To the Teacher

PURPOSE

The *Multiple Skills Series* is a nonconsumable reading program designed to develop a cluster of key reading skills and to integrate these skills with each other and with the other language arts. *Multiple Skills* is also diagnostic, making it possible for you to identify specific types of reading skills that might be causing difficulty for individual students.

FOR WHOM

The twelve levels of the *Multiple Skills Series* are geared to students who comprehend on the pre-first- through ninth-grade reading levels.

- The Picture Level is for children who have not acquired a basic sight vocabulary.
- The Preparatory 1 Level is for children who have developed a limited basic sight vocabulary.
- The Preparatory 2 Level is for children who have a basic sight vocabulary but are not yet reading on the first-grade level.
- Books A through I are appropriate for students who can read on grade levels one through nine respectively. Because of their high interest level, the books may also be used effectively with students functioning at these levels of competence in other grades.

The **Multiple Skills Series Placement Tests** will help you determine the appropriate level for each student.

PLACEMENT TESTS

The Elementary Placement Test (for grades Pre-1 through 3) and the Midway Placement Tests (for grades 4–9) will help you place each student properly. The tests consist of representative units selected from the series. The test books contain two forms, X and Y. One form may be used for placement and the second as a posttest to measure progress. The tests are easy to administer and score. Blackline Masters are provided for worksheets and student performance profiles.

THE BOOKS

This third edition of the *Multiple Skills Series* maintains the quality and focus that have distinguished this program for over 25 years. The series includes four books at each level, Picture Level through Level I. Each book in the Picture Level through Level B contains 25 units. Each book in Level C through Level I contains 50 units. The units within each book increase in difficulty. The books within a level also increase in difficulty— Level A, Book 2 is slightly more difficult than Level A, Book 1, and so on. This gradual increase in difficulty permits students to advance from one book to the next and from one level to the next without frustration.

To the Teacher

Each book contains an **About This Book** page, which explains the skills to the students and shows them how to approach reading the selections and questions. In the lowest levels, you should read About This Book to the children.

The questions that follow each unit are designed to develop specific reading skills. In the lowest levels, you should read the questions to the children.

In Levels A and B, the question pattern in each unit is
1. Title (main idea)
2. Stated detail
3. Stated detail
4. Inference or conclusion
5. Picture clue

The **Language Activity Pages** (LAP) in each level consist of four parts: Exercising Your Skill, Expanding Your Skill, Exploring Language, and Expressing Yourself. These pages lead the students beyond the book through a broadening spiral of writing, speaking, and other individual and group language activities that apply, extend, and integrate the skills being developed. You may use all, some, or none of the activities in any LAP; however, some LAP activities depend on preceding ones. In the lowest levels, you should read the LAPs to the children.

In Level B, each set of Language Activity Pages focuses on a particular skill developed through the book:

First LAP	Details
Second LAP	Picture interpretations
Third LAP	Main ideas
Last LAP	Inferences and conclusions

SESSIONS

The *Multiple Skills Series* is an individualized reading program that may be used with small groups or an entire class. Short sessions are the most effective. Use a short session every day or every other day, completing a few units in each session. Time allocated to the Language Activity Pages depends on the abilities of the individual students.

SCORING

Students should record their answers on the reproducible worksheets. The worksheets make scoring easier and provide uniform records of the children's work. Using worksheets also avoids consuming the books.

Because it is important for the students to know how they are progressing, you should score the units as soon as they've been completed. Then you can discuss the questions and activities with the students and encourage them to justify their responses. Many of the LAPs are open-ended and do not lend themselves to an objective score; for this reason, there are no answer keys for these pages.

When you read a story, you read words and sentences that belong together. They all help to tell about one **main idea**. Read this story. Think about what it is mainly about.

> Ann had a green plant. It began to look brown. She gave her plant water. She put it in the sun. Soon the plant was green again.

Do all of the sentences in the story tell about Ann's plant? Would "Ann's Plant" be a good title for the story? Figuring out what a story is mainly about is an important reading skill.

Another important reading skill is remembering the facts, or **details**, in a story. In the story above, what was the girl's name? What was wrong with her plant? A good reader pays attention to the facts.

A good reader also figures out **things that the writer does not say**. What did Ann do for her plant? Why do you think she did these things? The story does not tell you that green plants need water and sunlight, but you can figure this out from what the story tells you. Good readers think about what the story tells them. They figure things out as they read.

Sometimes a story has a **picture** to go with it. The picture may tell you things that the words do not. The picture can help tell the story.

In this book, there are twenty-five stories. Read each story and look at the picture that goes with it. Then choose a good **title**, or name, for the story. Answer the questions about what the story and the picture tell you.

Edna lives near a large lake. One day a car stopped and a man asked, "Do you have any worms to sell? I want to go fishing." Edna told the man she didn't have any worms. Soon other people stopped and asked for worms. Edna told them she didn't have any worms.

Then Edna thought, "If I dig up some worms, I can sell them." Edna began working. She dug up many worms. Other people stopped for worms. Edna sold the worms for three cents each. Soon she had made over five dollars.

1. The best title is—

   (A) Edna Goes Fishing

   (B) Edna Makes Money

   (C) A Beautiful Lake

   (D) A Large Fish

2. Edna lives near a large—

   (A) school   (B) store

   (C) lake   (D) park

3. To make money, Edna sold—

   (A) fish   (B) water

   (C) lemonade   (D) worms

4. You can tell that people go to the lake to—

   (A) fish   (B) swim

   (C) wash clothes   (D) paint pictures

5. In the picture, there is a—

   (A) bird   (B) car

   (C) bike   (D) flower

The children in Miss Ling's class are not like most children. They don't watch TV!

Miss Ling asked her class not to watch TV for one week. She told them that they could have more fun doing other things. The children said, "Let's find out if Miss Ling is right." Instead of watching TV, they read, made things, and played games with their families.

The children had so much fun that they are not going to watch TV for a year. Would you like to stop watching TV?

1. The best title is—

    (A) A Good TV Show

    (B) A Class Builds a Wagon

    (C) Children Have Fun Without TV

    (D) Miss Ling Buys a New TV

2. Miss Ling asked her class not to—

    (A) sleep   (B) eat

    (C) read books   (D) watch TV

3. The story says that the children—

    (A) played games   (B) went swimming

    (C) grew plants   (D) watched TV

4. Miss Ling is a—

    (A) doctor   (B) teacher

    (C) farmer   (D) child

5. In the picture, Miss Ling is—

    (A) playing a game   (B) running away

    (C) holding a book   (D) painting a house

Mike and his dog, Chipper, were walking in a woods. It was winter and snow was falling. Suddenly, Mike slipped and hurt his leg. He couldn't walk.

Soon night came. Mike was getting colder and colder. Then Chipper lay down on top of Mike. The dog kept him warm.

The next day, Mike's father found him. He had been in the woods all night. If Chipper had not kept him warm, Mike would have died. His dog had saved his life.

1. The best title is—

    (A) Mike Teaches His Dog a Trick

    (B) A Boy Is Saved by His Dog

    (C) A Dog Runs Away

    (D) A Boy Has Fun in the Snow

2. When Mike got hurt, it was—

    (A) raining   (B) snowing

    (C) hot   (D) fun

3. The dog saved Mike by keeping him—

    (A) warm   (B) awake

    (C) afraid   (D) cold

4. You can tell that Chipper is a—

    (A) tiny dog   (B) good pet

    (C) mean animal   (D) lazy dog

5. In the picture, you can see—

    (A) flowers   (B) animals

    (C) snow   (D) food

Mrs. Green lives in a home for older people. In the same place is a day-care room. It is for children who are too young to go to school. They come here while their moms or dads work. Each morning Mrs. Green helps out at the day-care room.

Sometimes, Mrs. Green gives a baby a bottle or rocks a baby to sleep. At other times, she reads stories to the children and plays games with them. Mrs. Green likes to be busy. She loves being with children, and the children love Mrs. Green too.

1. The best title is—

    (A) Children Like to Play Games

    (B) Mrs. Green Helps Children

    (C) Mothers Work Hard

    (D) Mrs. Green Sits Alone

2. Mrs. Green helps by—

    (A) singing songs   (B) painting pictures

    (C) reading stories   (D) writing letters

3. Mrs. Green loves—

    (A) dogs   (B) children

    (C) TV   (D) plants

4. You can tell that Mrs. Green feels—

    (A) happy   (B) sad

    (C) angry   (D) sick

5. In the picture, Mrs. Green is—

    (A) feeling sad   (B) sleeping

    (C) holding a baby   (D) reading a book

Lee cannot walk or run. She sits in a chair that has wheels. Lee can move the chair slowly. Sometimes people push her chair. When the children play games at school, Lee watches and cheers. One day the class was playing T-ball. This game is like baseball, but you hit a ball off a stick with your bat.

One day Pat said, "I want Lee to play on my side." Everyone was surprised. Sue said, "How can Lee play T-ball? She can't run."

Pat gave Lee a bat. Lee hit the ball off the stick. Pat pushed Lee in her chair with wheels as fast as he could. Pat and Lee reached first base before the ball. Everyone shouted.

1. The best title is—

    (A) Children Play Games

    (B) Chairs with Wheels

    (C) Lee Plays T-ball

    (D) Lee Is Not Happy

2. The story says that Lee cannot—

    (A) talk   (B) write

    (C) run   (D) cheer

3. Pat wanted to—

    (A) fix Lee's chair   (B) let Lee play T-ball

    (C) have a party   (D) play tag

4. The children had not asked Lee to play T-ball before because—

    (A) she did not know how to play

    (B) she could not see

    (C) she could not run

    (D) they did not like her

5. In the picture, you can see—

    (A) that Lee is angry   (B) a teacher

    (C) trees   (D) that Lee is happy

Ms. Ross took the letters from the mailbox and went into her house. She put the letters behind the TV set. Ms. Ross has to hide her mail—because her dog eats it!

Topper is a very big dog. Ms. Ross feeds him a lot of dog food every day, but Topper is always hungry. One day, Ms. Ross left a dollar on the table. Topper ate it. Another time, she left the mail on a chair. Topper ate that too!

Now Ms. Ross hides her money and the mail.

1. The best title is—

    (A) Making Money

    (B) A Hungry Dog

    (C) Watching TV

    (D) Cleaning a Table

2. Ms. Ross hid the mail—

    (A) in a book   (B) in a bottle

    (C) under a chair   (D) behind a TV set

3. Topper is a—

    (A) big cat   (B) small dog

    (C) big dog   (D) tiny horse

4. Ms. Ross hides the mail to keep it—

    (A) wet   (B) safe

    (C) small   (D) old

5. In the picture, you can see—

    (A) letters   (B) money

    (C) people   (D) a TV

A. Exercising Your Skill

Look at the words in the box below. They name some parts of your body. On your own paper, write the sentences and fill in the blank line with a word from the box.

legs	hands	eyes	ears

1. I use my _____ to write.
2. I use my _____ to hear the phone ring.
3. I use my _____ to walk where I want to go.
4. I use my _____ to read a book.
5. I use my _____ and _____ to watch TV.

B. Expanding Your Skill

In the story for Unit 5, you read about Lee. She could not use her legs. But Lee could hit a ball. Draw the boxes below on your paper. In each box write something a person *can* do.

If you can't use your legs, you can	If you can't see, you can

Tell your classmates if you know anyone who cannot walk, see, or hear. Talk about what that person can do. Tell why that person is special. Tell what you do with this person.

C. Exploring Language

Look at the lists below. All the things in one list are alike. Pick a list. Write the list on your paper. Add three more words to the list. Then write or tell about one thing on the list. Tell what it looks like, where you find it, and what it is used for.

Things You Can Ride In or On
plane   car   bike
____   ____   ____

Things You Can Play With
bat   ball   marbles
____   ____   ____

D. Expressing Yourself

Do one of these things.

1. Read the story in Unit 3 again. Pretend you are a person who writes for a newspaper. You made the notes below to tell what happened.

   Who? Mike
   What? fell and hurt his leg; couldn't walk
   Where? in the woods
   When? on a snowy day
   Who helped? Chipper, a dog
   How? kept Mike warm until help came

   On your own paper, use the notes to help you write a story for the newspaper. Write in sentences.

2. Fold drawing paper into four boxes. Draw something you can do well in each box. For each box, write a sentence. Tell what parts of your body you use to do that thing.

Jim and Tom were camping near a woods. They had brought a big bag of fruit to eat. When the fruit was almost gone, Jim put the bag near a tree.

An hour later, the boys heard a funny sound. They looked and saw a baby bear. It had smelled the fruit and put its head into the bag. The bag was stuck on its head!

The baby bear tossed its head and finally got rid of the bag. Then the bear ran into the woods. It wanted to find an easier way to get food!

1. The best title is—

    (A) Two Hungry Boys

    (B) Lost in the Woods

    (C) Two Boys Go Hunting in the Woods

    (D) A Bear Gets Stuck in a Bag

2. The boys in the story went—

    (A) swimming   (B) camping

    (C) driving   (D) flying

3. After the bag was off the bear's head, the bear—

    (A) climbed a tree   (B) sat down

    (C) ran to the boys   (D) ran into the woods

4. The bear put its head into the bag to—

    (A) hide   (B) sleep

    (C) eat the fruit   (D) look funny

5. In the picture, you can see—

    (A) three boys   (B) a fishing pole

    (C) a bear   (D) a tent

Paula likes to ride in a cart pulled by her horse. One day her neighbor, Mrs. Brook, asked, "Will you take me to work every morning?" Paula said she would. Mrs. Brook pays her a dollar each day for the ride.

Soon other people saw Mrs. Brook riding in Paula's cart. They wanted to ride to work in the cart, too. Now Paula makes many trips taking people to work every morning.

Paula likes giving people rides in her cart. It's fun, and she is also making money.

1. The best title is—

   (A) A Fast Horse

   (B) Driving a Car

   (C) Paula and Her Cart

   (D) Mrs. Brook Runs Home

2. Paula gives Mrs. Brook a ride—

   (A) home   (B) to work

   (C) to the store   (D) to a farm

3. Paula's cart is pulled by a—

   (A) cow   (B) car

   (C) dog   (D) horse

4. When Paula rides in her cart, she is—

   (A) afraid   (B) happy

   (C) sad   (D) tired

5. In the picture, the girl has—

   (A) a puppy   (B) a book

   (C) a stick   (D) two dollars

Kim lives in the city. Her house is on the third floor of a tall building. She likes to look out the window and watch the busy street. One day she saw Karen on the sidewalk.

Karen called up to her, "Kim, can you play with me in the park?"

Kim asked her mother. Mother said, "Yes, but please stop at the store on your way back and buy some eggs and milk." She gave Kim money.

Kim and Karen had fun playing in the park. On the way home, they stopped at the store. Kim likes living in a city. She can walk almost everywhere she needs to go.

1. The best title is—

    (A) Kim Lives in a City

    (B) Kim's House

    (C) The Park

    (D) A Tall Building

2. The story says that Kim likes to—

    (A) play jump rope   (B) read

    (C) watch the busy street   (D) swim

3. Mother wanted Kim to—

    (A) clean her room   (B) buy eggs and milk

    (C) stay home   (D) read

4. Kim and Karen will probably—

    (A) eat apples together   (B) play together again

    (C) move away from   (D) never go to the
        the city   park again

5. In the picture, Kim and Karen are—

    (A) riding their bikes   (B) jumping rope together

    (C) inside the building   (D) walking on the
                                    sidewalk

"My window is broken again," Maria told her father. Her father went into her bedroom. He put a new piece of glass in her window. Maria's window is by a tree where many birds live. Almost every week a bird would fly into the window and break it.

Maria asked herself, "What can I do to stop the birds from breaking my window?" Then she had an idea. The birds flew into the window because they couldn't see it. Maria painted pictures on her window. Then the birds were able to see the window. It has not been broken since Maria painted the pictures.

1. The best title is—

   (A) A Pet Bird

   (B) Birds and Maria's Window

   (C) Maria Learns to Paint Pictures

   (D) Buying a Piece of Glass

2. The story says that Maria's window is by a—

   (A) park   (B) barn

   (C) field   (D) tree

3. Maria's window was broken by—

   (A) flying birds   (B) angry dogs

   (C) stones   (D) rain

4. You can tell that the birds—

   (A) moved to another tree   (B) can see the pictures

   (C) like to sing   (D) cannot fly

5. In the picture, you can see a—

   (A) happy girl   (B) sad father

   (C) broken window   (D) new window

Mr. Green loves to eat. One day he said, "I am too heavy. I'm going to stop eating so much."

During the day, Mr. Green didn't eat very much. But at night he would forget and go to the refrigerator to get food. Then he bought something that helps him remember not to eat too much. He bought a "talking" refrigerator!

When Mr. Green opens the refrigerator door, a voice says, "Remember not to eat." The talking refrigerator has helped Mr. Green stop eating too much.

1. The best title is—

   (A) Mr. Green Goes Shopping

   (B) A Man and His Garden

   (C) A Talking Refrigerator

   (D) A Broken Door

2. The story says that Mr. Green loves to—

   (A) run   (B) eat

   (C) sleep   (D) paint

3. The refrigerator talks when Mr. Green—

   (A) hits it   (B) washes it

   (C) closes the door   (D) opens the door

4. Mr. Green wants to get—

   (A) fatter   (B) thinner

   (C) shorter   (D) lost

5. In the picture, the man is holding a—

   (A) bag   (B) glass

   (C) box   (D) toy

Carla has a job that she likes very much. Every day she takes newspapers to her neighbors' houses. Most girls and boys ride bikes when they carry newspapers. Carla does not have a bike, but she has something else to ride—her horse, Rags.

Carla's neighbors like it when she rides Rags to their houses. Not many people get their newspapers from a girl riding a horse. She throws the paper onto the porch and rides to the next house.

Carla likes her job. She also likes riding Rags each day.

1. The best title is—

    (A) Writing Funny Stories

    (B) Carla and Her Horse

    (C) A New House

    (D) A Lost Bike

2. The name of Carla's horse is—

    (A) Jumper   (B) Pal

    (C) Rags   (D) Racer

3. The story says that Carla does not have a—

    (A) hat   (B) turtle

    (C) horse   (D) bike

4. Carla's neighbors like her to come to their houses because it is—

    (A) different   (B) slower

    (C) sad   (D) not nice

5. In the picture, you can see—

    (A) books   (B) newspapers

    (C) houses   (D) doorbells

A. Exercising Your Skill

Close your eyes. Picture a city in your mind. If you do not know what a city looks like, look at the picture in Unit 9. Then copy the two headings and the numbers on your own paper. On each numbered line write a thing you see or hear in the city.

What I See in the City	What I Hear in the City
1. _____	1. _____
2. _____	2. _____
3. _____	3. _____
4. _____	4. _____

Share your list with a classmate. Tell what you know about the city. Do you live in or near a city? If you live in a city, share what you like most and least about the city. If you do not live in a city, but you have visited one, tell what you did there. If you have not been to a city, tell about one you want to visit.

B. Expanding Your Skill

Look at the picture of the city in Unit 9. Write the sentences below on your own paper. Fill in the blank line with a word that tells about living in a city.

1. Kim lives in a _____ building.
2. Kim saw Karen from her _____ .
3. A bus came down the _____ street.
4. Kim and Karen walked to the _____ .
5. They walked from the park to the _____ .
6. At the store they bought _____ .
7. Kim's _____ needed the eggs.

C. Exploring Language

Look at the picture in Unit 9. It shows two girls walking down a city street. The story tells us that the girls are going to the park. Write a story that tells what the girls do at the park. First picture a park in your mind. Copy the sentence about Kim and Karen on your own paper. Then finish the story. Tell what the girls saw and did at the park.

Kim and Karen walked to the city park.

D. Expressing Yourself

Do one of these things.

1. Read this riddle about a place.

    I see many planes. There are many people with suitcases. I hear loud roars as planes take off. I am going to a place far away with my family. I feel excited. Where am I?

    Did you guess that this is an airport? Now think of a place you can tell about. Close your eyes and picture this place. Then, on your own paper, write about this place, but do not tell its name. Let a classmate guess where you are (your riddle). Tell what you see, hear, or smell. Tell why you are there and how you feel. Tell what time of year it is. Remember, do not name the place. Make up your own riddle.

2. Tell what city you live in or near. Find a map. Find the city on the map. Ask your teacher to help you. Pick a place on the map to visit. Write about that place. Tell where it is. Then tell how you will get there.

For many years, Gordon fixed bikes. Then one day he thought, "I'm going to take a long bike ride." He got on his bike and rode across the whole country.

Since then, Gordon has ridden his bike across the country nine times. On one trip, he rode nine thousand miles in 220 days. Gordon rides his bike so much that he is called "The Bicycle Man."

Sometimes, Gordon takes his dog, Sassy Girl, with him. She rides in a basket on the bike. Maybe Sassy Girl should be called "The Bicycle Dog"!

1. The best title is—

    (A) Fixing Bikes

    (B) A Short Trip

    (C) The Bicycle Man

    (D) A Lost Dog

2. Gordon has ridden across the country—

    (A) nine times   (B) ten times

    (C) with his cat   (D) on a horse

3. The story says that Gordon—

    (A) is a doctor   (B) fixed bikes

    (C) sleeps all day   (D) flew kites

4. You can tell that Gordon—

    (A) has a brother   (B) cannot walk

    (C) likes to ride a bike (D) knows how to fish

5. In the picture, you can see a—

    (A) tie   (B) dog

    (C) coat   (D) hat

Some girls are named Rose after the beautiful flower. Other girls are named after the warm months of May and June. Mr. and Mrs. Champlin named their baby daughter after a town!

When Mr. and Mrs. Champlin's baby was born, they didn't know what to name her. Then Mr. Champlin said, "Remember the town called Dania that we visited on our vacation? It was a pretty town. Let's call our daughter Dania."

Mrs. Champlin thought it was a good idea. Were you named after some object or some place? It might be interesting to find out!

1. The best title is—

   (A) A Beautiful Garden

   (B) The Champlins Take a Vacation

   (C) How a Girl Got Her Name

   (D) A Long Trip Home

2. The story says that Dania is a—

   (A) large city   (B) small river

   (C) noisy town   (D) pretty town

3. The story says that the Champlins have a—

   (A) son   (B) daughter

   (C) new car   (D) pet

4. Dania was named after a—

   (A) place   (B) plant

   (C) song   (D) story

5. In the picture, you can see—

   (A) four people   (B) two cars

   (C) a bus   (D) a bridge

When Carlos was only five years old, he went to see a circus. He loved it so much that he said, "When I grow up, I am going to work in a circus."

Carlos is now grown up and he does work in a circus. He trains lions and tigers. The people clap when Carlos has the animals sit on high chairs. Sometimes he has the wild animals jump over his head.

If you go to the circus, look for a man who works with lions and tigers. It may be Carlos!

1. The best title is—

   (A) Carlos Works in a Circus

   (B) Catching Wild Animals

   (C) What Lions Eat

   (D) Carlos the Clown

2. The story says that Carlos trains—

   (A) horses   (B) tigers

   (C) fish   (D) elephants

3. Sometimes Carlos has the animals—

   (A) chase each other   (B) jump over his head

   (C) drive a car   (D) sing songs

4. When Carlos has the animals sit on high chairs, the people—

   (A) run away   (B) become angry

   (C) hate it   (D) like it

5. In the picture, there are—

   (A) elephants   (B) dogs

   (C) lions   (D) horses

Mrs. Tedoca is a doctor who does not help people. Mrs. Tedoca is a doll doctor.

Many children get dolls as presents. Sometimes the dolls get broken. Mrs. Tedoca has learned to fix broken dolls so they look like new. She can put new hair on a doll and fix broken arms and legs. She can even paint new faces on dolls.

Mrs. Tedoca calls her store "Tedoca's Doll Hospital." Everyone says that Mrs. Tedoca is the best doll doctor in town.

1. The best title is—

    (A) A Beautiful Doll

    (B) Mrs. Tedoca Breaks a Leg

    (C) A Doll Doctor

    (D) Birthday Toys

2. Mrs. Tedoca makes broken dolls look—

    (A) ugly   (B) sad

    (C) like new   (D) very old

3. Mrs. Tedoca calls her store—

    (A) Tedoca's Toy Store   (B) A Doll Hospital

    (C) Tedoca's Pet Hospital   (D) Tedoca's Doll Hospital

4. Mrs. Tedoca makes many children—

    (A) happy   (B) angry

    (C) cry   (D) work

5. In the picture, the doll has a broken—

    (A) leg   (B) arm

    (C) back   (D) head

Mika and his grandfather went for a walk. The rain had stopped. The sun was just coming from behind the clouds. Mika pointed to the sky and said, "Wow, what a beautiful rainbow! I wonder what makes a rainbow."

"I can tell you," said Grandfather. "After it rains, the air is full of tiny drops of rain, but we can't see them. Then the sun comes out and shines through the drops of water. The drops break up the sun's light into violet, indigo, blue, green, yellow, orange, and red."

"That is good to know," said Mika, "but I will always think of a rainbow as a painting in the sky."

1. The best title is—

   (A) Going for a Walk

   (B) A Rainy Day

   (C) Rainbows in the Sky

   (D) A Sunny Day

2. A rainbow is—

   (A) one color   (B) many colors

   (C) no color   (D) clouds

3. A rainbow shows in the sky when the sun—

   (A) shines through rain   (B) is behind a cloud

   (C) shines through smoke   (D) has set

4. You can tell that Mika felt—

   (A) very tired   (B) hungry for lunch

   (C) sad and lonely   (D) full of wonder

5. In the picture, the boy is pointing to—

   (A) his grandfather   (B) the moon

   (C) the rainbow   (D) the land

Mr. Garcia loves to fish. One day when he was fishing, a neighbor came to watch him. Mr. Garcia asked, "Don't you like to fish?" His neighbor, Lucy, said that she liked to fish but she didn't have a fishing pole.

The next day, Mr. Garcia spoke to the principal at Lucy's school. The principal let Mr. Garcia visit Lucy's class. He asked, "How many children like to fish but don't have a fishing pole?" Many children raised their hands. Mr. Garcia bought fishing poles and gave them to the children.

Now, when Mr. Garcia goes fishing, he has a lot of company.

1. The best title is—

    (A) A Man Buys Children Fishing Poles

    (B) Mr. Garcia Catches a Large Fish

    (C) A Girl and Her Pet Fish

    (D) What Fish Like to Eat

2. The story says that Mr. Garcia likes to—

    (A) eat   (B) run

    (C) fish   (D) read

3. At the school, many children needed—

    (A) TV sets   (B) new shoes

    (C) new coats   (D) fishing poles

4. You can tell that Mr. Garcia is a—

    (A) poor teacher   (B) kind man

    (C) young boy   (D) fast runner

5. In the picture, the children are—

    (A) on a bus   (B) in a school

    (C) by a lake   (D) on a street

Mail carriers have friends that they meet every day. It may be a dog, or it may be a girl or boy that always says hello. Barbara Baker is a mail carrier who has a bird as a friend.

Every morning when Barbara walks down Elm Street with the mail, the bird is waiting in a tree. As soon as the bird sees her, it flies down and sits on Barbara's shoulder. It sits there as she walks down the street putting letters into the mailboxes. Then it flies back to the tree and waits until Barbara comes again the next day.

1. The best title is—

    (A) A Lost Letter

    (B) A Mail Carrier's Friend

    (C) Writing to a Friend

    (D) At the End of the Day

2. Barbara's friend is a—

    (A) dog   (B) boy

    (C) bird   (D) cat

3. Barbara's friend waits for her—

    (A) in a tree   (B) in a cage

    (C) on the sidewalk   (D) on the ground

4. The bird in the story—

    (A) cannot fly   (B) can read

    (C) scares Barbara   (D) likes Barbara

5. In the picture, there is a—

    (A) mail truck   (B) mailbox

    (C) small car   (D) bird

A. Exercising Your Skill

Work with a classmate. Look at the pictures for Units 16 and 19. Each picture shows a person doing a job. Decide what that job is. Then talk about what the person does at the job. Tell if the job is hard work. Do many people do this job? Would you like to do this job? Next, name a job you would like to do. Tell your classmate what you will do in the job. Take turns with your classmate. If you know about another job, tell your classmate about that job. Listen well. Speak clearly.

B. Expanding Your Skill

The first list below has the heading The Job. The words in the list name different jobs. The second list has the heading The Work. The second list tells the work a person does at a job. Write ten sentences about jobs on your own paper. Use the two lists. First write one job from the list. Then write the words from the second list that tell about the job.

Example: 1. A dentist works on teeth.

The Job	The Work
1. dentist	works at a circus
2. teacher	takes pictures
3. fisher	helps people learn to read
4. clown	works in a kitchen
5. doctor	works on teeth
6. painter	catches fish
7. cook	flies an airplane
8. police officer	helps people who are sick
9. photographer	keeps people safe
10. pilot	paints houses

C. Exploring Language

Read the stories about workers. Each story has a main idea. The other sentences tell more about the main idea. If you think of a good title for the story, you will have found the main idea. Write a title for each story on your own paper.

1. Work on a farm keeps me busy. I make the ground ready for planting seeds. Corn, wheat, peas, and beans are the crops I grow. I take care of many animals. I have one horse, five pigs, and two hundred chickens. The chickens lay eggs. I carry the eggs to a store in my truck. People buy my eggs from the store. The other animals live in the barn. Cleaning the barn is not easy.

2. I drive a big truck. Today I am taking fruit from the farm to a store. Some stores are very far away. Sometimes I drive for many miles without stopping. Driving a truck is not easy. A truck driver must be careful. I always drive safely.

D. Expressing Yourself

Do one of these things.

1. Think about the workers in your town. Act out one of their jobs. Have a classmate or the class guess who you are. If they cannot guess, give them hints.

2. Make a "Workers' Book." Draw a different worker on each sheet of paper. Give each picture a title. Put all the pictures that you and your classmates draw together to make a book.

Jeff built a doghouse for his dog, Romper, but it does not look like most doghouses.

Romper often follows Jeff to school. So Jeff thought, "I'll make Romper his own school." He asked his father to help him. Together they built a doghouse that looks like the school Jeff goes to. It even has a bell on the top. When Romper is hungry, he pulls a rope and the bell rings. Then Jeff gives him something to eat.

Romper likes his new doghouse, but he still follows Jeff to school.

1. The best title is—

    (A) Teaching a Dog Tricks

    (B) Jeff Goes to School

    (C) Romper's New Doghouse

    (D) Playing with Romper

2. Jeff built the doghouse with—

    (A) a friend   (B) his father

    (C) his teacher   (D) his sister

3. The doghouse looks like a—

    (A) store   (B) garage

    (C) tent   (D) school

4. You can tell that Jeff probably—

    (A) never feeds Romper   (B) walks to school

    (C) hates dogs   (D) is an old man

5. In the picture, the dog is—

    (A) eating   (B) sleeping

    (C) chasing a ball   (D) pulling a rope

Mr. Lopez wanted to have a birthday party for his daughter, Rosa. He wanted a party that would be different from most birthday parties. Rosa loves to roller-skate, so Mr. Lopez gave Rosa a roller-skating party.

When the children came to Rosa's house for the party, Mr. Lopez put them into a bus. Then they rode to a building where people roller-skate. All the children were given roller skates to use. Many children had never skated before, so they fell down a lot. But everyone had a good time. Rosa said, "This is the best party I've ever had!"

1. The best title is—

    (A) A Long Bus Ride

    (B) Mr. Lopez Goes Swimming

    (C) A Roller-skating Party

    (D) A Big Cake

2. The story says that Rosa loves to—

    (A) play ball   (B) roller-skate

    (C) swim   (D) read

3. Everyone at the party—

    (A) got hurt   (B) cried

    (C) had a good time   (D) lost their skates

4. You can tell that Rosa—

    (A) liked to swim   (B) knew how to skate

    (C) owned a bus   (D) has a sister

5. In the picture, there are—

    (A) two boys   (B) no girls

    (C) no boys   (D) four people

Ben likes to run. He runs every day. Sometimes he goes ten miles. Running helps Ben stay in shape. He also likes to run in races.

Ben ran in one race that was almost thirty miles long. Many, many people ran in this race. The race started in a small town and ended in a big city. Ben and the others ran through the streets of three towns. They ran up and down hills. The people along the road shouted for them. "Keep going!" they said. It took Ben three hours to finish the race, and he was very tired. Ben did not win the race, but he was still proud of what he had done.

1. The best title is—

    (A) Ben's Boat Race

    (B) Ben's Bike Race

    (C) Ben Skates in a Race

    (D) Ben Runs in a Race

2. The race in which Ben ran was almost—

    (A) five miles   (B) ten miles

    (C) twenty miles   (D) thirty miles

3. When Ben finished the race, he was—

    (A) hungry   (B) surprised

    (C) very tired   (D) sad

4. Ben was proud of himself because—

    (A) he won the race   (B) he finished the race

    (C) his mother saw him   (D) he swam well

5. In the picture, people are racing—

    (A) in a city   (B) in the country

    (C) in the mountains   (D) over fields

There was going to be a parade at school. Miss Roads asked her class, "What can we do to be different from the other classes?" Betty had a good idea. She said that everyone in the class should dress up to look like an animal!

The class began working. They made clothes that looked like animals. When the children dressed in the clothes, they looked like lions, elephants, giraffes, and monkeys.

Everyone thought that Miss Roads' class was the best in the parade. It was funny to see the girls and boys dressed up as animals.

1. The best title is—

    (A) Children Watch a Very Long Parade

    (B) A Class Learns to Read

    (C) Children Dress to Look Like Animals

    (D) A Trip to the Zoo

2. The story says that some of the children looked like—

    (A) cows   (B) monkeys

    (C) horses   (D) tigers

3. The parade was held at a—

    (A) park   (B) library

    (C) store   (D) school

4. When people saw Miss Roads' class in the parade, they probably—

    (A) cried   (B) ran away

    (C) laughed   (D) were frightened

5. In the picture, you can see—

    (A) four people   (B) six people

    (C) two teachers   (D) one man

Everyone who sees the Sailor Circus likes it. The Sailor Circus is like other circuses, but it is put on by children.

There are 150 children in the Sailor Circus. They ride animals, train dogs, act like clowns, and do tricks. The circus also has a band to play music. There are thirty girls and boys in the band.

The Sailor Circus is held in a big tent that holds 2,500 people. The children love it when the people clap. How would you like to be in the Sailor Circus?

1. The best title is—

    (A) A Dog That Can Do Tricks

    (B) A Children's Circus

    (C) A Wonderful Game

    (D) A Funny Clown

2. The Sailor Circus is held—

    (A) on a boat   (B) in a school

    (C) in a building   (D) in a tent

3. The story says that the Sailor Circus has—

    (A) a band   (B) funny cars

    (C) 15 lions   (D) 20 monkeys

4. You can tell that some of the children in the circus—

    (A) get hurt   (B) act funny

    (C) fly airplanes   (D) sell food

5. In the picture, the young woman is—

    (A) sitting   (B) sleeping

    (C) high in the air   (D) on the ground

Charles Meryman is a doctor. But he is not a doctor who helps sick people. He helps fish.

People who live in Charles' town call him "The Fish Doctor." If their pet fish get sick, they call him on the telephone. Charles drives his truck to the people's houses. In the truck, he has medicine to help the sick fish get better.

Sometimes, Charles is called by a pet store when there are sick fish. Wherever he goes, "The Fish Doctor" is always welcome.

1. The best title is—

    (A) The Fish Doctor

    (B) Charles Goes Fishing

    (C) A New Pet Store

    (D) A Wonderful Meal

2. Charles goes to people's houses in a —

    (A) car   (B) bus

    (C) truck   (D) train

3. People telephone Charles when their—

    (A) dogs are sick   (B) fish are sick

    (C) cats are sick   (D) children are sick

4. You can tell that some people—

    (A) don't like Charles   (B) paint their fish

    (C) love their pet fish   (D) eat their pet fish

5. In the picture, you can see—

    (A) a boy   (B) a telephone

    (C) two trucks   (D) fish

A. Exercising Your Skill

In this book find a picture that shows a happy person. Read the story again to find out why the person is happy. Then find a picture that shows someone who is sad or angry. Read the story to find out why.

Talk with your class about feelings. When do you feel happy, sad, angry, or afraid? Tell why you feel that way. Listen well when someone is talking. When you talk, look at the person and talk clearly.

B. Expanding Your Skill

Read the sentences below. They tell about some of the stories you have read. Think how each person feels. On your own paper, write the word from the box that tells how the person feels. The words can be used more than once.

sad	excited	proud	angry

1. Ben finished a race that was almost 30 miles long. He felt _____ .
2. "My window is broken again," Maria told her father. She felt _____ .
3. Mike slipped and hurt his leg. He felt _____ .
4. Rosa said, "This is the best party I ever had." She felt _____ .
5. Lee's friends shouted, "Great hit," as she went to first base. Lee felt _____ .
6. A child broke her doll. The child felt _____ .
7. The doll doctor fixed the doll to look like new. The doctor felt _____ .

C. Exploring Language

Finish the story below. Copy the story on your own paper. Fill in the lines with words and sentences. The story will tell of a time you felt sad, happy, angry, afraid, or surprised.

One day I felt _____ . I felt that way because _____

_____ .

Other things that make me feel the same way are

_____ .

D. Expressing Yourself

Below are some stories from your book. Pick one. Copy it on your own paper. Write a different ending than the one in your book.

1. Ben ran in a long race. He was almost to the finish line when _____

_____ .

2. Paula gave people rides in her cart. She made money from this. One day Paula thought of a new way to make money. She _____

_____ .

3. Last week a bird broke Maria's window. Maria didn't want birds to break the window again. She thought of a new way to stop them. She _____

_____ .

4. Mike and his dog, Chipper, were walking in the woods. It was winter and snow was falling. Suddenly _____

_____ .